FUZZY FORENSICS

DNA Fingerprinting Gets Wild

ashby
Ashby BP
Publishing
For Nose Publishing

L. E. Carmichael, PhD

In memory of
Richard Servetnyk and Ralph Burt,
for giving animals a voice

Table of Contents

Before becoming a writer, I studied genetics—the science of DNA—for 11 years. For my PhD, I used DNA fingerprints to study wolves and arctic foxes in Canada's North. DNA fingerprints are easy to make, but have incredibly powerful uses. They reveal everything from family relationships among animals to how (and *why*) those animals travel around their environments. This information helps us protect and conserve wild species.

DNA fingerprints can also be used to solve crimes involving wildlife. As a forensic scientist, I have made fingerprints for 15 wildlife investigations. *Fuzzy Forensics* is the story of my favorite case. I hope you love it!

– L. E. Carmichael

Faces of the Case

Richard Servetnyk
- Conservation officer with Alberta Fish and Wildlife
- Led the investigation

Alice Wilson*
- Employee at Laughing Brook Ranch
- Witnessed and reported the crime

Lindsey Carmichael
- Forensic scientist at the University of Alberta
- Analyzed DNA fingerprints

Ralph Burt
- Veterinarian from the Canadian Food Inspection Agency
- Collected blood samples for DNA testing

* To protect their privacy, names of witnesses, suspects, and locations have been changed.

Chapter 1
The Case of the Kidnapped Elk

On August 25, 1999, Alice Wilson witnessed a crime. It was the start of breeding season on Laughing Brook Ranch, an elk farm north of Edmonton, in Alberta, Canada.

The last seasons' **calves** had to be separated from their mothers before the **hinds** could mate again. Using oats as bait, ranch hands lured the elk out of their grassy pasture and into a holding pen. From the pen, the noisy, jostling elk funneled into a series of narrowing corridors, eventually forming a single file. One by one, elk entered the **squeeze**, a device that kept them from squirming while the ranchers checked their health. Workers marked calves with large, plastic ear tags. Others would know from the tags that the elk belonged to the farm. Finally, young elk exited into the calf pasture, while hinds and **stags** went to a second pasture for breeding.

Elk pass through narrow corridors on their way to the squeeze.

Old MacDonald Had an Elk

Elk meat is very low in fat, making it healthier than beef. Many people hunt for elk in the wild, but game ranches and farms also produce elk meat. The first elk ranch in Alberta opened in 1977. As of October 2013, there were 12,688 elk living on a total of 197 ranches around the province. Ninety percent of these ranches are found in the Peace River, Lakeland, Buck Lake, Edmonton, and Red Deer areas.

Across Canada, game ranches can be found in Saskatchewan, Manitoba, Ontario, and Quebec. Elk are the most popular species, but red deer, white-tailed deer, fallow deer, mule deer, reindeer, moose, and bison are also raised for food.

Scientists call elk *Cervus elaphas*. Shawnee Indians call them *wapiti*, which means "white rump."

Ranchers use large plastic ear tags to identify their elk.

Wilson worked on the farm. Her job was to record information about each elk as it came through the squeeze. The law requires elk ranchers to report every animal living on their farms, so these records had to be correct. When an adult female, or hind, elk wearing ear tag 154 entered the squeeze, Wilson knew there was a problem. The ear tag was small and metal, not large and plastic. Hind 154 was a wild animal.

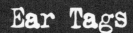

Ear Tags

Biologists study animals using markers such as leg bands, tattoos, GPS collars, and even fur color or fin shape. The first animals marked with ear tags were probably arctic foxes in 1935. Today, ear tags allow biologists and ranchers to easily identify individual elk from a distance without disturbing the animal. Metal tags are used for wild elk. Plastic tags are used for farm elk.

Ear tags are very similar to the dangly earrings a person might wear. One end has a sharp point and the other end has a slot. Ranchers push the point through the elk's ear and secure it by inserting the point into the slot. A skilled worker can do this quickly, causing very little pain to the animal. Once applied, the tag has no effect on the elk's behavior or survival.

An endangered burrowing owl marked with leg bands.

Scientists mark butterflies using permanent ink pens.

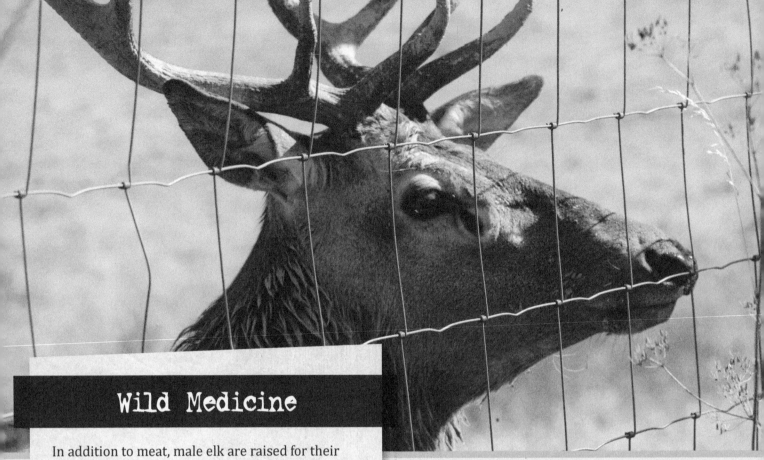

Wild Medicine

In addition to meat, male elk are raised for their antlers, which drop off and regrow every year. During growth, a soft fuzz, called velvet, coats the bone. This velvet antler phase lasts from March to June. The average stag grows 6.4 to 6.8 kilograms (14 to 15 lbs) of antler every year.

Powdered velvet antler has been used as a traditional Chinese medicine since at least 168 BCE. Recent research shows that eating velvet antler may improve healing and reduce swelling in sore joints. In 2005, scientists tested whether velvet antler could help dogs with **arthritis**. Sixty days after starting the treatment, the dogs were more active and placed more weight on their bad legs. If further research supports this result, elk antler might become a good alternative to painkillers such as ibuprofen.

Wilson knew that it's illegal for wild animals to be held captive on game farms. She mentioned Hind 154 to Terrence Steppke, the ranch's owner, right away. But instead of holding the elk and calling Alberta Fish and Wildlife, Steppke released the animal into his breeding pasture. Then he told Wilson not to add the wild elk to the Laughing Brook Ranch records.

The next animal to enter the squeeze was a male calf. Wilson thought the calf belonged to the wild hind, but Steppke gave it a plastic ear tag with the number 9957. He told Wilson to record Calf 9957 as a captive baby that had been born on the ranch.

These discs cut from antlers will be ground to powder and used as traditional medicine.

Wilson obeyed, but she couldn't stop thinking about the wild elk. Chuck Hewitt, Wilson's boyfriend, also worked at Laughing Brook Ranch. She asked him for some advice. To her shock, Hewitt told her he'd seen the two elk outside the ranch's fence a few days earlier. He knew they were wild, because they weren't wearing the plastic ear tags that ranch farmers use. That's when Hewitt opened the gate and chased them onto the ranch, adding the wild animals to Steppke's captive herd.

Wilson had to make a choice. If she stayed quiet, she could keep her job and her boyfriend. If she told, she could help the elk.

On September 19, 1999, Wilson chose the elk. She called the Report A Poacher hotline and reported the crime.

Elk calves do not have antlers.

Richard Servetnyk

Richard Servetnyk was born on August 28, 1952 in Saskatoon, Saskatchewan. He joined Alberta Fish and Wildlife as a conservation officer in 1974, eventually becoming the manager of the Major Investigations and Intelligence Unit. Known for his leadership, kindness, and passion for protecting Alberta's wild species, Servetnyk was named Officer of the Year in 2003. He accepted the award on behalf of all of the officers on his team.

When asked why he worked so hard defending wildlife, Servetnyk always replied, "Because I really like ducks." He passed away in 2010.

Jasper National Park, Alberta - the original home of Hind 154.

The Investigation Begins

The Laughing Brook Ranch elk-napping was not the first crime Wilson had reported. "She'd given us accurate information in the past," said Richard Servetnyk, the conservation officer who interviewed her after her call to Report A Poacher. "I had a feeling she was telling the truth about this."

Servetnyk worked for Alberta Fish and Wildlife, a branch of the government. As a conservation officer, his job was to make sure elk ranches did not affect wild elk. Before Servetnyk could charge Steppke with a crime, however, he needed hard evidence to support Wilson's testimony.

Servetnyk knew that Alberta government biologists used metal ear tags to study wild elk. He asked them for information about Hind 154. According to the biologists, she had been marked in Jasper National Park the previous February. That month, the biologists had moved her and 49 other hinds to the Slave Lake area to start a new wild herd. At the time, Hind 154 did not have a calf, but was probably pregnant.

Servetnyk reasoned that sometime after the baby was born, "Calf and mom decided they didn't like the Slave Lake area and wandered south." This made sense, because other elk from the Slave Lake herd had traveled as far as Athabasca and Morinville.

Wild elk live in groups, so Hind 154 was probably attracted to Laughing Brook Ranch by the pungent scent and squealing **bugles** of the captive herd. But how did the two get in, when the fence surrounding the farm was 3 metres (10 ft) high? "I don't think they jumped," Servetnyk said.

Wilson's story and Servetnyk's findings gave reasonable grounds to believe laws had been broken. On October 22, a local judge issued a search warrant. It gave Servetynk permission to look for the hind and calf on Laughing Brook Ranch.

Search Warrants

A search warrant gives police or conservation officers permission to enter a person's property or business to look for evidence of a crime. To get a warrant, officers have to explain what crime they suspect has occurred, list what types of evidence they are looking for, and specify where they plan to look. Judges use this information to ensure the reasons for the search warrant are reasonable. Reasonable grounds are very important. If officers do not have reasonable grounds, any evidence found during a search could be thrown out of court during a trial.

Servetnyk had been a conservation officer for 26 years before the case of the kidnapped elk. In that time, he'd performed more than 100 searches using warrants.

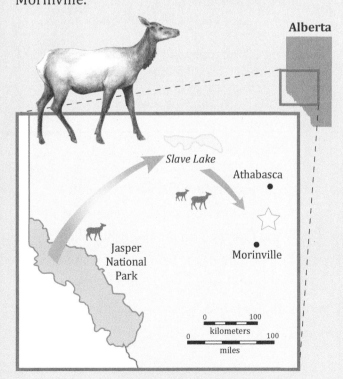

Alberta

Slave Lake

Athabasca

Jasper National Park

Morinville

0   100
kilometers
0   100
miles

These farmed elk stags are beginning to regrow their antlers.

Dr. Ralph Burt

Dr. Ralph Burt was born in Maidstone, Saskatchewan, on August 27, 1938. He had 20 years' experience as a veterinarian when he joined the Canadian Food Inspection Agency in 1982.

Game farming was just beginning in Alberta at that time. Every day was a new challenge for Burt, who cared most about the safety of the animals. His favorite part of the job was educating ranchers and promoting the proper care of elk, deer, and bison. By the time Burt retired in 2005, he'd devoted more than 40 years of his life to this goal.

"Ralph was a kind man who enjoyed nature and helping animals," his wife Linda said in 2013. "Day or night—it didn't matter when the call came in—he was on his way." Dr. Burt passed away in 2009.

Search and Rescue

At 10:00 a.m. on October 25, 1999, Servetnyk presented his warrant at Laughing Brook Ranch. Three other conservation officers, three elk biologists, a veterinarian from the Canadian Food Inspection Agency, a farm inspector from Alberta Agriculture, and a forensic computer specialist from the Royal Canadian Mounted Police (RCMP) joined Servetnyk for the search. They needed to find the computer with the Ranch's records. They also needed to find two specific elk within Steppke's whole herd.

"I've had a lot of experience with warrants on game farms," Servetnyk said, "and they are difficult to execute." Elk are large animals. If they're frightened, they can injure themselves or the people around them. To ensure the elk's safety, the biologists and veterinarian Dr. Ralph Burt supervised the search. "We were lucky," Servetnyk said. "It went off without a hitch."

Using the squeeze, it took Servetnyk's team approximately 20 minutes to find and separate Hind 154 and Calf 9957 from the other elk. But Steppke claimed he didn't know Hind 154 was on his farm. He also insisted that Calf 9957 had been born on Laughing Brook Ranch and therefore belonged to him.

Adopt-An-Elk

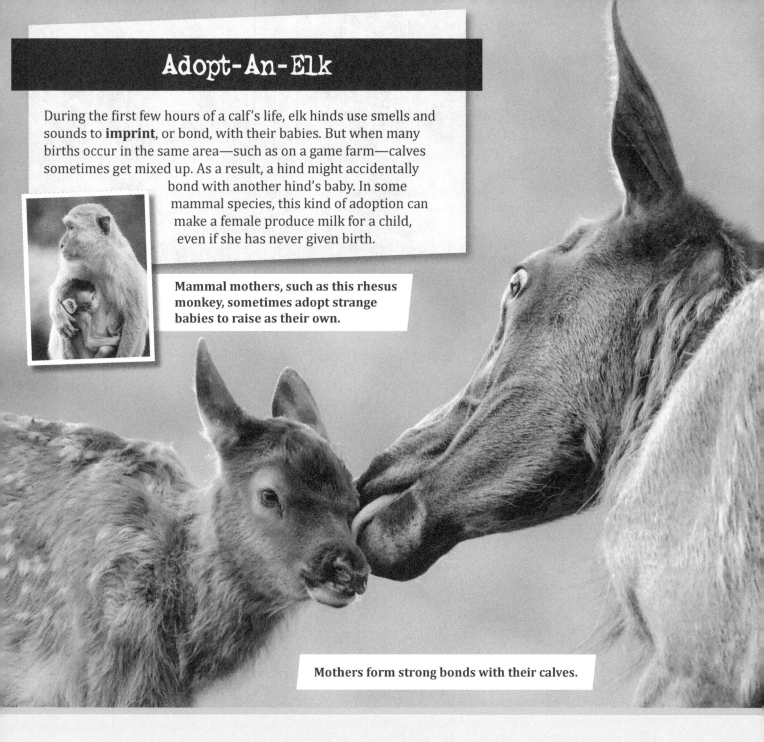

During the first few hours of a calf's life, elk hinds use smells and sounds to **imprint**, or bond, with their babies. But when many births occur in the same area—such as on a game farm—calves sometimes get mixed up. As a result, a hind might accidentally bond with another hind's baby. In some mammal species, this kind of adoption can make a female produce milk for a child, even if she has never given birth.

Mammal mothers, such as this rhesus monkey, sometimes adopt strange babies to raise as their own.

Mothers form strong bonds with their calves.

Dr. Burt could see that the hind and the calf were very comfortable around each other. In his opinion, they behaved as mother and child. That wasn't enough, though, because Burt also knew that hinds sometimes adopt strange calves to raise as their own.

"In the past," Burt said, "the only way to tell whether an elk calf belongs to a certain mother, was to be there when it's born." But thanks to modern **forensic science**, there is now another way—a way using DNA.

It's the Law

Three separate laws regulate Alberta elk ranching. They are:

The Livestock Industry Diversification Act (LIDA)

Alberta Agriculture is the branch of government responsible for enforcing LIDA. This law defines a game farm animal as a member of a wildlife species that is:

- Ear-tagged
- In captivity
- Registered with the government

The Wildlife Act

The Wildlife Act defines hunting as chasing, harassing, capturing, injuring, or killing a wild animal. It also defines situations in which these activities are legal, and when they are not. The Wildlife Act protects wild animals of the same species as game farm animals. At the time of this case, Alberta Fish and Wildlife enforced this law. Today, conservation officers work for Alberta Justice and Solicitor General.

The Health of Animals Act

This law protects the health and well-being of captive animals and helps prevent diseases from spreading from food products to people. It's enforced by the Canadian Food Inspection Agency, whose officers visit game ranches every three to five years to ensure laws are obeyed.

Who knew science could taste this good?

Beans in a Bag: Counting Animals Using Marks

Biologists use marks, like ear tags, to understand how animals move in their environments, how they interact with other animals, and how long they live. Marks can also help scientists estimate population size— the number of animals of a wild species that live in a particular area. This experiment shows how to use marks to count jellybeans!

What You Need

- *Brown paper bag*
- *Chip or paper clip*
- *3 cups popped popcorn*
- *1/2 cup red jellybeans*
- *10 blue jellybeans*
- *Notebook and pencil*

The Best Kind of Mark

The best wildlife marks are permanent, clearly visible, and don't affect or harm the animal in any way. DNA fits all of these requirements, and many biologists now use it. DNA information is present in animal hair. Animals are marked when they leave their hairs behind on tree bark or barbed wire. They're recaptured when biologists find hair with matching DNA at another place or time.

A tuft of bear hair snagged on a barbed wire trap in northwest Montana. These hairs will be used as a source of DNA for mark-recapture studies.

What You Do

① — Pour the popcorn and red jellybeans into the bag.

The popcorn represents leaf litter on a forest floor. The red jellybeans represent beetles.

② — Seal the bag with the clip and shake it to mix.

③ — Open the bag. Stick your hand inside and <u>capture</u> ten red jellybeans by taking them out of the bag.

④ — Place ten blue jellybeans in the bag. The blue jellybeans represent <u>marked</u> beetles.

Record the number of beetles and how you marked them in your notebook.

⑤ — Seal the bag and shake it to mix. This mimics the way beetles move around in their environment.

⑥ — Open the bag. Without looking, stick your hand inside and <u>recapture</u> ten jellybeans.

Record how many are red and how many are blue.

⑦ — The proportion of marked beetles in your recapture should be close to the proportion of marked beetles in the entire bag. Because of this relationship, you can use the recapture formula to estimate the total number of beetles in the population.

⑧ — Following the example in the sidebar, use the recapture formula to make your estimate. Record these numbers in your notebook.

⑨ — Empty the bag and count all of the jellybeans. Compare this number with your estimate. How accurate was your estimate?

Recapture Formula

Total number of beetles in bag =

$$\frac{(\text{Number of marked beetles} \times \text{Number of beetles recaptured})}{\text{Number of recaptured beetles that were blue}}$$

Example:
If you recaptured 4 blue jellybeans and 6 red ones, your calculation would look like this:

Total number = (10 x 10) /4

The answer is an estimate of 25 beetles in the entire bag.

In addition to ear tags, two of these elk are wearing radio collars, which help scientists find the animals in the wild.

In the Real World

Mark-recapture experiments are more complicated when living animals are involved. How might estimates change if:

- The marks fell off or washed away?

- The marking process harmed some animals, which died before recapture?

- Animals moved in or out of the area between capture and recapture?

- Biologists cheated by deliberately recapturing marked animals?

Biologists attach a leg band to a young osprey, to learn more about the bird's behavior and movements.

Chapter 2
DNA Detective Hits the Lab

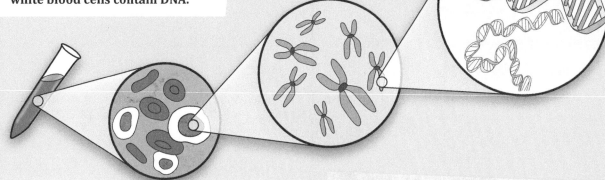

There are two types of blood cells, red and white. In mammals, only white blood cells contain DNA.

DNA stands for deoxyribonucleic acid. All living things have DNA. It controls hair color, gender, and whether or not animals will get certain diseases. Because it's so powerful, DNA is sometimes called the instructions for life.

Almost every **cell** in an animal's body contains DNA. Biologists use DNA from skin, muscle, hair roots, feathers, bones, and teeth to learn about wildlife. Forensic scientists—those who use science to help solve crimes—also rely on information from DNA. Just as every human being has unique fingerprints, every living thing has unique DNA. Using "DNA fingerprints," forensic scientists can correctly match people or animals to pieces of biological evidence found at crime scenes.

Double Trouble: Twins and DNA

Every animal has a unique DNA fingerprint—unless the animal is an identical twin. Identical twins come from a single fertilized egg. That means their DNA is identical. Around four out of every 1,000 human births are identical twins. Human twins sometimes cause problems for forensic scientists. It is impossible tell which sibling left DNA at the scene of a crime.

Biologists have found identical twins in medaka fish, domestic pigs and horses, dogs, and wolves. Less than 1 percent of elk are born as twins. No one knows how many of these twins are identical. As with humans, some twins are fraternal twins. That means they are born from two different eggs and therefore have different DNA.

Which of these twins is guilty?

DNA can also reveal family relationships. Within cells, DNA strands are twisted into tightly coiled packages called **chromosomes**. Animals normally have a pair of each type of chromosome. When animals mate, each parent passes one chromosome from every matching pair to the baby.

That's why Dr. Burt took blood samples from Hind 154 and Calf 9957 during the search of Laughing Brook Ranch. If the elk really were mother and child, they would share half of their chromosomes. To find the truth in the DNA, Servetnyk's team needed a forensic scientist.

A calf's DNA is a mixture of chromosomes inherited from both of its parents.

Lindsey Carmichael in a genetics laboratory.

DNA Fingerprints

Lindsey Carmichael worked as a biologist at the University of Alberta. She specialized in using DNA to study the movements and behavior of animals in the wild. When Richard Servetnyk asked for her help with the case of the kidnapped elk, she agreed immediately.

"To that point, I'd only done forensic testing for **poaching** cases," Carmichael recalled, "cases where animals had been killed. I loved the idea of helping animals that were still alive."

Carmichael received the elks' blood samples on March 15, 2000. She immediately began constructing a DNA fingerprint for each animal.

"Fingerprinting takes advantage of the unique shape and sequence of DNA," Carmichael said. DNA is a two-stranded **molecule** that looks a bit like a twisted ladder. Pairs of chemicals, called bases, form the ladder's rungs. Each type of base—G, C, A, and T—has a slightly different shape. Their shapes can only fit together two ways. G always pairs with C, and A always pairs with T.

The order of the bases along the DNA strands has a meaning, just like the order of words in a sentence. "The important thing for forensics," Carmichael explained, "is that we can compare the base sequences between individuals. If we look at the same location in each animal's chromosomes, the base order often differs between them."

The Chain of Custody

Investigators store physical evidence in bottles, bags, or boxes. Each container is labeled with the date, time, and location of where the evidence was found. This record also contains a description of the evidence and a unique identification number, forming the first link in the item's chain of custody. Whenever that piece of evidence is handled, the record is updated with the date and time, who touched the evidence and why, and whether any part of the item was changed or removed.

These records must be accurate and complete, because they prove that no one could have tampered with the evidence. Problems with the chain of custody could mean the evidence can't be trusted and it may not be used in court.

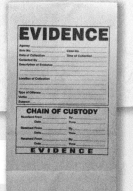
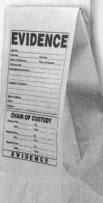

Chain of custody information can be recorded directly on the evidence bag.

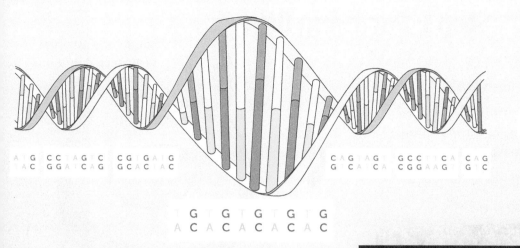

AIGCCIAGIC CGIGAIG
TACIGGAICAG GCACIAC

CAGIAGI GCCITCA CAG
GICAICA CGGAAGI GIC

GIGIGIGIG
ACACACACAC

How many repeats does this microsatellite contain?

In some areas of the chromosomes, DNA bases are arranged in repeating sequences, like ACACACACAC. These repeats are called **microsatellites.** They are especially useful for forensics, because the number of repeats varies between animals. One elk, for example, might have a chromosome with 75 ACs in a row, for a total length of 150 bases. A second elk might have only have 70 repeats, or 140 bases, for the same microsatellite. That means forensic scientists do not have to capture the entire DNA sequence base by base. They can tell the difference between animals just by looking at the lengths of their microsatellites.

A DNA fingerprint is a collection of length measurements for a set of microsatellites. To create fingerprints for the kidnapped elk, Carmichael had to follow three steps.

Forensic evidence, like this bullet, is the strongest type of evidence.

A World of Evidence

Criminal investigations use both soft and hard types of evidence. Soft evidence is weaker and less trustworthy than hard evidence.

Examples of soft evidence include:

- **Hearsay:** A report of what someone else said. Hearsay is often called second-hand evidence.

- **Circumstantial Evidence:** This type of evidence suggests a link between the suspect and the circumstances surrounding a crime. Circumstantial evidence shows that a person could be guilty, but doesn't prove he or she is.

Examples of hard evidence include:

- **Direct Evidence:** First-hand eyewitness testimony.

- **Physical Evidence:** Sometimes called real or forensic evidence, this could include:

  - Threads and fibers
  - Paint
  - Broken glass
  - Bullets or weapons
  - Soil
  - Fingerprints or shoe impressions
  - Blood, hair, bone, meat, or other sources of DNA

Step 1: Purifying DNA

Blood is a mixture of liquid and cells. The cells protect an animal's DNA and also contain **molecules** such as fats and proteins. To examine the elk's DNA, Carmichael first had to separate it from all the other parts of their blood. This first step of DNA fingerprinting is called **purification**.

Here's how it works:

Within the cell, DNA is protected by a second barrier, called the nucleus.

1. **Enzymes** are proteins that assist with chemical reactions. One type helps breaks down the protective **membranes** surrounding DNA. Carmichael added these enzymes to a small volume of each elk's blood. Elk DNA leaked out of the broken cells and into the liquid.

2. Carmichael moved the blood mixture into a tube called a column. It had a space for liquid and a paper filter. It also had a hole in the bottom. She placed the column in a laboratory machine that spins at high speed. Spinning created a force that pulled liquid and most of the molecules out through the hole. The DNA, however, got stuck to the filter.

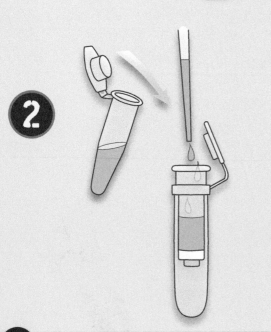

SPIN

3

3. Carmichael washed the stuck DNA with liquid rubbing alcohol. This rinsed away any leftover cell debris.

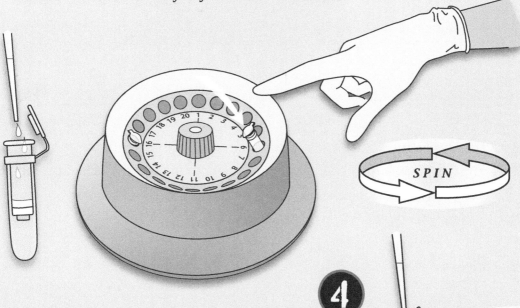

SPIN

4

SPIN

4. Lastly, Carmichael added a liquid that dissolves DNA. This lifted it off the filter. A final spin of the machine pulled the DNA out of the column and into a storage tube. The pure elk DNA was now ready for the second step in the fingerprinting process.

Inventing DNA Fingerprints

Sir Alec Jeffreys, a British scientist, wanted to understand how DNA differs from person to person. In 1984, he was working on a method for viewing many repeat sequences from a person's DNA at the same time. His first experiment compared DNA from a group of relatives.

When he checked his results, on September 10, Jeffreys discovered what looked a bit like supermarket barcodes. He immediately noticed that each person's barcode was unique, but similar to those of their relatives. "It was an absolute Eureka moment," Jeffreys said. "It was a blinding flash." Quite by accident, he had invented the first method of DNA fingerprinting.

Two years later, Jeffreys helped police investigate the murders of two young girls. His team made DNA fingerprints for more than 4,000 men and found one killer. On January 23, 1988, Colin Pitchfork became the first man to be convicted of a crime based on DNA evidence.

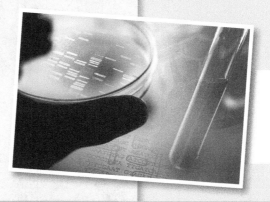

Jeffrey's original DNA fingerprints looked a lot like the glowing lines showed here.

Step 2: Making More Microsatellites

One animal's chromosomes can contain billions of DNA bases. But microsatellite sequences used by forensic scientists contain less than 300 bases. Finding one to measure is like finding a specific grain of sand in an entire sand castle.

To increase their chances of finding the right microsatellite, scientists use a process called the **polymerase chain reaction** (PCR). PCR is like a photocopier for DNA. It makes millions of copies of the desired microsatellite. It ignores all other sequences in the DNA. When complete, microsatellite copies vastly outnumber the other sequences. This makes them much easier to find. PCR is the second step in DNA fingerprinting.

Here's how it works:

Pure elk DNA dissolved in liquid. This came from the purification process.

Short pieces of DNA called primers. On a DNA strand, microsatellite repeats are surrounded by unique base sequences. Primers match these sequences on either side.
One primer in each pair is attached to a marker molecule that glows under light.

Loose DNA bases—the building blocks for microsatellite copies.

An enzyme that builds DNA.

Carmichael placed the tube into a machine that heats and cools the liquid mixture.

First, the machine heated the liquid to 94°C (201°F). Heat broke the bonds between the bases. This separated the DNA strands.

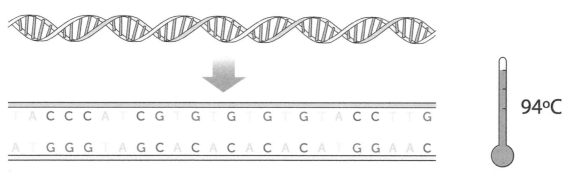

TA C C C A T C G T G T G T G T G T A C C T T G
A T G G G T A G C A C A C A C A C A T G G A A C

94°C

The machine cooled down to 54°C (129°F). In the liquid, primers bonded with matching sequences of the elk DNA.

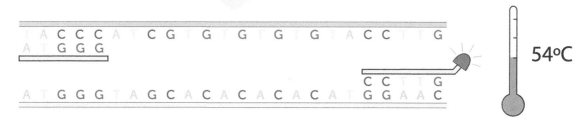

54°C

When the temperature increased to 72°C (162°F), enzymes attached to the primers. They zipped along the strands, adding loose DNA bases. This created new DNA strands. They were perfect copies of the original microsatellites.

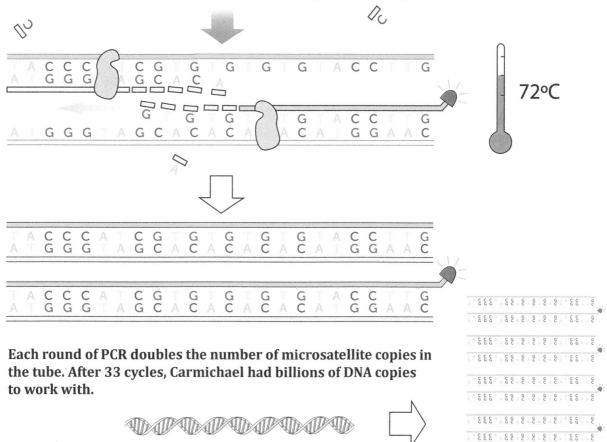

72°C

Each round of PCR doubles the number of microsatellite copies in the tube. After 33 cycles, Carmichael had billions of DNA copies to work with.

Step 3: Seeing Sizes

Carmichael used PCR to copy seven different microsatellites for each elk. DNA is very small, though. Billions of microsatellite copies fit inside just 20 µl of liquid. That is 1/250th of a teaspoon.

It is impossible to measure microsatellites with the naked eye. To finish the DNA fingerprints, Carmichael needed to complete the third and final step. She used a process called **electrophoresis** to separate the microsatellites and make them visible. Electrophoresis means "carried by electricity."

Here's how it works:

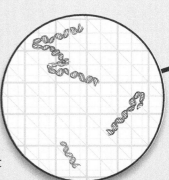

DNA molecules have an electrical charge. This charge is negative. Because of this, DNA moves away from the negative end of an electrical current. This is similar to the way the negative ends of magnets repel each other.

During electrophoresis, an electrical current forces microsatellite DNA to travel through gel, a certain kind of chemical. Gel is a bit like a knitted sweater. It looks solid, but is made of tiny strands separated by holes. Short pieces of DNA pass through the holes more easily than longer pieces. That means they can travel faster. It's a bit like a large dog trying to chase a kitten through a pet door. The kitten shoots through, but the dog has to wiggle.

CRITTER CASES

Science Takes the Stand

Scientists began testing DNA fingerprinting as a tool for wildlife forensics in 1989. On March 1, 1991, Canadian biologist Dr. Bradley White became the first person in North America to present DNA evidence for a wildlife court case.

Four men from Ontario were accused of killing a deer outside of hunting season. White compared DNA from blood found at the kill site to DNA from a deer's head found in the suspects' boat. At the trial, White testified that the DNA fingerprints from both samples matched. This proved that the deer in the boat had been shot at the kill site.

However, DNA could not prove when the deer had been shot, so the judge found the suspects not guilty of hunting out of season. This first case, however, proved that DNA could help solve wildlife crimes. It's been used ever since.

In the 0.2 mm gap between two sheets of glass, Carmichael made a gel 36 cm (14 in) long. She placed the gel into an electrophoresis machine. Next, she loaded small samples of each elk microsatellite into wells at the top of the gel.

Bradley White founded the Wildlife Forensic DNA Laboratory at Trent University in 1989. It is the oldest lab in North America that specializes in DNA fingerprinting for wildlife crimes. Since it opened, the lab's forensic scientists have helped solve at least 1,000 cases. More than 90 percent of these crimes happened in Canada.

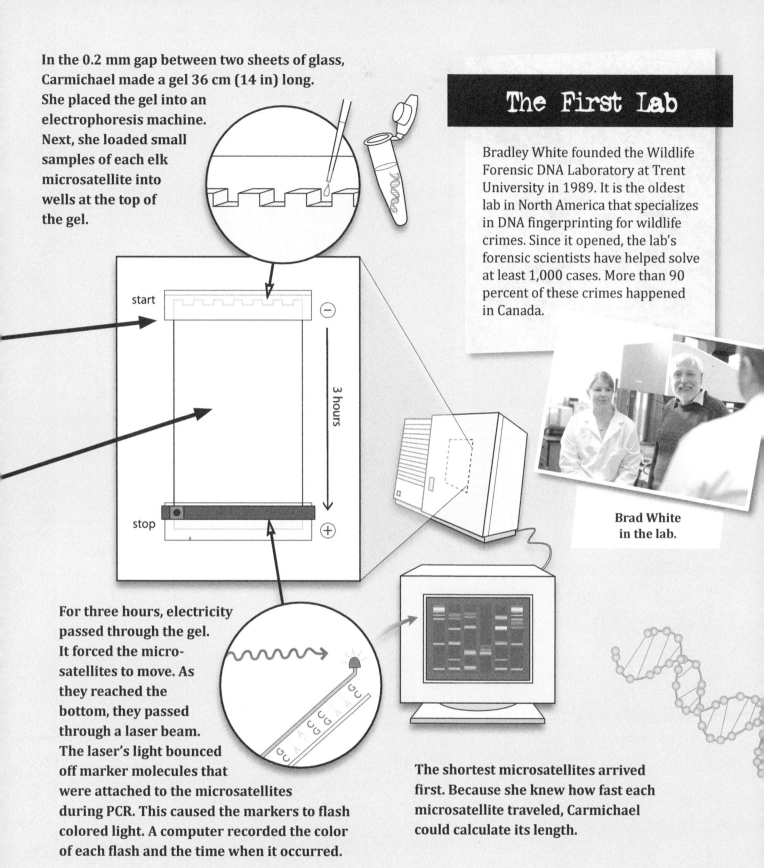

start

3 hours

stop

Brad White in the lab.

For three hours, electricity passed through the gel. It forced the micro-satellites to move. As they reached the bottom, they passed through a laser beam. The laser's light bounced off marker molecules that were attached to the microsatellites during PCR. This caused the markers to flash colored light. A computer recorded the color of each flash and the time when it occurred.

The shortest microsatellites arrived first. Because she knew how fast each microsatellite traveled, Carmichael could calculate its length.

Each elk had two copies of the seven microsatellites Carmichael measured. One copy came from the elk's mother and one from its father. Therefore, each completed DNA fingerprint included 14 different measurements. It was time to find out whether Hind 154 and Calf 9957 shared any DNA.

EXPERIMENT 2

Genes in a Jar: Purifying Plant DNA

Carmichael needed complex and expensive equipment to see elk DNA during her investigation. Some plants have so much DNA, however, no equipment is needed. Try this experiment to purify DNA from wheat plants.

> **WARNING**
> This experiment uses rubbing alcohol, and the fumes can hurt your nose. Check with an adult before you begin.

Everything you need to purify DNA!

What You Need

- *Small jar with lid (a spice jar works well)*
- *Measuring spoons*
- *Watch or timer*
- *Raw wheat germ (your source of plant DNA)*
- *Hot water*
- *Liquid dish soap*
- *Rubbing alcohol*
- *Toothpicks (optional)*

How This Works

The hot water and shaking motion soften the wheat germ cells. This makes them easier to break open. When the dish soap breaks the cells, DNA escapes into the surrounding water. Because water dissolves DNA, you still can't see it.

DNA does not dissolve in rubbing alcohol, however. Any DNA that touches the alcohol layer becomes solid and visible.

What You Do

1. — Measure 2 teaspoons of wheat germ into the jar. Add 3 tablespoons of very hot water.

2. — Cap the jar tightly and shake it for three minutes. Then let the jar sit for ten minutes.

3. — Add 1 teaspoon of dish soap to the jar. Gently tip the jar back and forth for five minutes. Don't shake too hard! If soap bubbles form, you're probably breaking the DNA strands.

4. — Tilt the jar. Slowly pour 2 tablespoons of rubbing alcohol down the jar's inner edge. You want the alcohol to form a layer on top of the wheat germ mixture.

Make sure the alcohol forms a layer on top of the liquid already in the jar.

5. — Slowly swirl the contents of the jar. Do not let the layers mix. Do you see the white, stringy goo where the layers meet? That is the wheat germ's DNA! To take a closer look, lift it out of the jar with a toothpick.

What Next?

Try using cool water instead of hot or powdered dish soap instead of liquid. Do you see more or less DNA?

Next, repeat the original experiment using a different kind of plant. Starting with a small piece of fruit, like kiwi or banana, follow the same process. If fruit produces less DNA, how could you modify the experiment to get a better result?

Chapter 3

The Case Goes to Court

DNA fingerprints of parents and children are similar in a very specific way. One copy of a child's microsatellite is the same size as one copy of its mother's microsatellite. The child's second copy matches one of its father's sizes. These matches occur at every microsatellite in a DNA fingerprint. When Carmichael compared the fingerprints of Hind 154 and Calf 9957, she found this pattern right away.

Hind 154 did not adopt Calf 9957, as Steppke had claimed. The hind was the calf's real mother. That meant both elk were wild.

With DNA fingerprinting, Dr. Burt's expert opinion, and Alice Wilson's eyewitness testimony, Officer Servetnyk had proof that crimes were committed on Laughing Brook Ranch.

He was ready to present the evidence in court.

CRITTER CASES

The Poisoned Lamb

Egyptian vultures are endangered in Spain, where only 38 breeding pairs survive. It is illegal to kill these birds, even though they sometimes hunt farmers' lambs.

In 2007, Spanish conservation officers found the body of an Egyptian vulture next to the body of a lamb. Both had been poisoned. Officers suspected the lamb's owner had killed it so that vultures would die after feeding on the lamb's remains.

Egyptian vultures are normally scavengers, but sometimes kill live prey.

Using DNA fingerprints, forensic scientists proved that the lamb's parents were sheep from a certain shepherd's flock. Officers charged the shepherd with killing the vulture. As of December 2013, the case was still in court.

	Microsatellite Names (letters) and Sizes (numbers)													
	A		B		C		D		E		F		G	
Hind 154	226	230	229	231	169	171	150	154	132	134	191	195	122	122
Calf 9957	218	230	229	231	169	171	150	154	132	134	191	197	120	122

Hind 154 and Calf 9957 share at least one size at every microsatellite. This proves they are mother and child.

An elk calf drinks its mother's milk in the mountains of Colorado.

Teaching an Old Lab New Tricks

Alberta Fish and Wildlife's Forensic Laboratory was founded in 1973 by Bob McClymont and Sandra Drummond. DNA fingerprinting wasn't available at that time. When the technology first developed, the only lab with the right equipment was at the University of Alberta. The case of the kidnapped elk was one of the last forensic investigations done at the University.

In 2000, Rick Jobin launched Alberta Fish and Wildlife's DNA Laboratory. Jobin says that for him, the best part of the job is the variety. "We perform research, collect evidence, analyze DNA, perform post-mortem examinations, train officers, and provide expert witness testimony in court," he said. "This wide variety of responsibilities keeps things fresh."

Her Majesty the Queen
v.
Terrence Steppke and Laughing Brook Ranch

The trial began on January 17, 2001, in Fort Saskatchewan, Alberta. There was a lot at stake for Steppke. If he were convicted of all the charges, he would lose his license to run a game farm for six to ten years. Laughing Brook Ranch would be out of business.

Steppke's trial did not involve a jury. A judge made all the decisions.

Based on Servetnyk's evidence, the government of Alberta charged Terrence Steppke and his ranch with three crimes:

The case against Steppke was so strong, his only chance of winning was to have the evidence thrown out of court. To do this, Steppke's

1. **Capture of two wild animals.**
   Under the Wildlife Act, capturing animals is an illegal form of hunting.

2. **Possession of wildlife with intent to traffic.**
   Illegal sale of wildlife is called trafficking. Because the ranch sold elk meat and velvet antler, the law assumed Steppke's motive was to make more money by expanding his herd.

3. **Failure to notify.**
   Steppke should have contacted Alberta Fish and Wildlife as soon as he found out that wild animals were on his ranch. Keeping the animals secret was a crime, even if Steppke didn't catch them personally.

A white-tailed deer.

Forensic Facts:
Wildlife Crime in Alberta

- Between 70 and 90 wildlife forensic investigations happen in Alberta each year. About 80 percent of them involve DNA evidence. **A moose.**

- Moose and white-tailed deer are the most common victims of wildlife crime.

- About 10 percent of the time, DNA proves that human suspects are innocent.

- Only about 5 percent of wildlife cases ever go to court. The rest of the time, suspects make deals to receive lesser sentences.

lawyer tried to prove Servetnyk had no reasonable grounds for searching Laughing Brook Ranch. Without reasonable grounds, all evidence from the search—including the DNA fingerprints—would be lost.

Servetnyk spent six long hours on the witness stand, answering questions about his investigation. "Steppke had a very good lawyer," Servetnyk recalled in 2008. "He really grilled me." Despite the stress, Servetnyk only lost his cool once—when the lawyer implied he might have altered the facts to get the warrant.

After the day's testimony, Judge Marshall spent the night considering the case. On the morning of January 18, he announced his decision: reasonable grounds existed. All of the evidence against Steppke could be presented in the trial. Steppke's lawyer immediately arranged a deal. Steppke pled guilty to failure to notify and the other charges were dropped. The judge ordered Laughing Brook Ranch to pay a fine of $4,000.

The lawyers agreed to end Steppke's trial in exchange for a plea bargain.

The case of the kidnapped elk was finally closed.

Case Timeline

From start to finish, the case of the kidnapped elk lasted almost two years.

1999

February 15, 1999
Biologists move Hind 154 from Jasper National Park to Smokey Lake.

August 25, 1999
Alice Wilson discovers the wild elk on Laughing Brook Ranch.

September 19, 1999
Wilson calls Report A Poacher to describe the crime.

October 8, 1999
More witnesses come forward to support Wilson's story.

October 22, 1999
Officer Servetnyk receives a search warrant for Laughing Brook Ranch.

October 25, 1999
Servetnyk's team conducts the search and Dr. Ralph Burt collects blood for DNA testing.

2000

March 15, 2000
Lindsey Carmichael receives the blood samples and begins making DNA fingerprints.

2001

January 17–18, 2001
The case is tried in an Alberta Court. Steppke admits that he is guilty of one charge in the case.

Loki's curly fur is a sign he might not be a pure chocolate lab.

Which Pups Are Pure?: Fingerprints and Family

Imagine you're a forensic scientist. A woman has just called you about her puppy, Loki. The breeder claimed Loki was a pure chocolate lab, but his fur is suspiciously long and curly. When confronted, Loki's breeder confessed that Loki's mother escaped after mating. There's a chance the mother mated with a second male dog before she came home.

Using five microsatellites, you make DNA fingerprints for the mother dog, Loki, and the other puppies in Loki's litter: Odin, Thor, Freya, and Syn. You also make a fingerprint for the chocolate lab thought to be the puppy's true father. You know that dogs have two copies of each microsatellite, and therefore a maximum of two microsatellite sizes. You also know that every puppy inherits one copy of each microsatellite from its mother and one from its father.

Here are the microsatellites you discovered:

Dog's Name	Microsatellite Names (letters) and Sizes (numbers)									
	A		B		C		D		E	
Mother	121	125	230	232	176	180	149	157	201	209
Chocolate Male Lab	125	127	228	234	176	182	151	155	203	207
Odin (puppy)	121	127	228	230	176	180	149	155	203	209
Loki (puppy)	121	123	230	232	176	184	153	157	201	207
Thor (puppy)	123	125	230	232	176	184	149	151	205	209
Freya (puppy)	125	125	230	234	180	182	149	155	201	207
Syn (puppy)	123	125	226	230	176	178	151	157	205	209

Pure bred labradors come in three colors, golden, black, and chocolate brown, but all three types have short, straight fur.

(1) — Compare each puppy's microsatellite sizes to those from its mother. Mark the copy that the mother passed to each pup. Follow the example shown for Odin.

(2) — Compare the remaining microsatellite sizes to the DNA fingerprint of the male lab. Can this dog be Loki's father? Is he the father of the other puppies?

(3) — Do you believe that Loki is a purebred chocolate lab?

(4) — Based on these results, which microsatellite sizes belong in the DNA fingerprint of the second, mystery father?

Turn to page 68 to check your answers!

A pure bred chocolate lab puppy.

CRITTER CASES

Puppy Fraud

Baby animals from the same litter can be related in different ways. Some may be identical twins, and some just brothers and sisters. Occasionally, animals from the same litter are half-brothers or half-sisters. They have the same mother, but different fathers. Scientists call this situation multiple **paternity**. It occurs in many mammal species, but is only a forensic issue is cases like Loki's. Pet breeders who charge purebred prices for mixed-breed puppies are committing the crime of fraud.

By December 31, 2012, the American Kennel Club had used DNA fingerprinting to test the parentage of more than 110,000 puppies. In 2012, they found 59 litters with multiple paternity.

Do you believe that these Dachshund puppies all have the same father?

Chapter 4
Science Saving Wildlife

The case of the kidnapped elk was over. But people commit crimes against wildlife every day—all over the world. DNA fingerprinting is a powerful tool for forensic scientists investigating these cases.

Christopher Kyle is a biologist who sometimes works at the Wildlife Forensic DNA Laboratory in Ontario. "Many people don't realize how broad the field of wildlife forensics really is," Kyle said. "We've handled cases ranging from poaching [illegal hunting] to animal abuse to trade in endangered species, and for almost any kind of question, we can find an answer using DNA."

Forensic scientist Christopher Kyle at work.

No Girls Allowed

In Alaska, it is legal for Native Americans to hunt polar bears. However, hunters are encouraged to harvest male bears only. This guideline protects mother bears, who give birth to cubs and protect them while they grow. If too many females are killed, fewer cubs will be born and polar bear populations will shrink.

Hunters have to report the sex of any bears they kill, but conservation officers can't double-check these reports if the animals have already been butchered. Instead, the officers collect meat samples that forensic scientists use as DNA sources. To test the bears' sex, scientists use a DNA sequence called SRY. SRY is found in male mammals, but not females.

These tests show that hunters misreport the sex of their bears 14 percent of the time. In most of these cases, hunters claimed the bears were male when they were actually female. Many of these errors are probably honest mistakes, but it's also possible that some hunters lie about their kills.

CRITTER CASES

Animal skins and other products earn traffickers huge profits on the black market.

This rhinoceros from Zimbabwe, Africa, was probably poached for its horns, which are used in traditional medicine.

Trade involves selling live animals or products made from dead animals. Illegal trade is known as trafficking. After habitat destruction, it is the second-largest threat to endangered animal species around the planet. Trafficking affects 33 percent of threatened mammal species, 30 percent of threatened bird species, and 6 percent of threatened amphibian species. Millions of wild animals are captured, injured, or killed by traffickers every year.

Interpol (International Criminal Police Organization) estimates that illegal trade in wild species is worth more than US$20 billion every year. It's more profitable than smuggling guns or selling illegal drugs. Wildlife traffickers know that their chances of being caught are very small. They also know that jail terms and monetary fines for smuggling wildlife are lower than for other types of organized crime. These risks are nothing compared to the money traffickers can make.

CUSTOMS
CUSTOMS INSPECTION STATION

When they cross international borders, smugglers have to sneak wildlife products past customs officials.

Wildlife trafficking is a global problem, and fighting it requires international cooperation. As of 2014, 180 countries have signed the Convention on International Trade in Endangered Species of Wild Fauna and Flora (CITES). The countries' governments have agreed to protect endangered species by cracking down on wildlife traffickers.

The first step to stop trafficking is to catch smugglers who attempt to bring animals or wildlife products (such as leather, fur, or dried meat) across borders. But smugglers can't be charged without proof that the species they are transporting are protected by CITES.

In the past, identifying a species was very challenging. This was especially true if smugglers carried products rather than whole animals. Today, forensic scientists can purify DNA from a wide range of parts and products. By looking for DNA sequences unique to only one type of plant or animal, scientists can identify an unknown species. If the product was made from an endangered species, the smuggler can then be charged with trafficking.

Sniffer dogs are used to detect illegal goods at airports and border crossings.

When they lose their fear of people, bears and other predators often become dangerous.

DANGER

Area closed due to bear
DO NOT ENTER

Secteur fermé-présence d'ours
ACCÈS INTERDIT

Scat Attack

In most wildlife investigations, animals are victims. But when predators attack people, DNA evidence can identify the furry criminal.

In September, 1999, an animal killed a man near Dease Lake, in northern British Columbia. Conservation officers shot a male black bear they believed was guilty. They asked Lindsey Carmichael to prove it using DNA.

Normally, forensic scientists compare DNA from an animal with DNA from blood or hairs left at a crime scene. In this case, the only evidence the bear had left behind was scat… also known as poop!

Compared to tissue, blood, and hair, scat is a bad source of DNA. It's full of bacteria and chemicals that break DNA into tiny pieces that are too small to be copied by PCR. "I couldn't find any microsatellites," Carmichael said. "But there was enough DNA to prove the scat came from a male black bear." With other evidence from the scene, it was enough to close the case.

Shell Shock: Identifying Endangered Birds

There are 359 different types of parrots and cockatoos, many of which are protected under CITES. Because these birds are beautiful and intelligent, they are also very popular pets. Some collectors pay tens of thousands of dollars to purchase a single endangered parrot. As a result, exotic birds are common targets for wildlife traffickers.

A specially-designed shirt used for smuggling parrot eggs.

Traffickers capture parrots from their native habitats and smuggle them into countries around the world. Instead of hatched birds, which are harder to hide, traffickers smuggle eggs. They use special padded vests that fit under their clothing. The vests protect the eggs and keep them warm during transport.

In most cases, law enforcement officers can't identify a bird's species by looking at an egg. DNA from eggshells can be used to make fingerprints, though. In 2012, forensic scientists tested the DNA of 90 bird eggs smuggled into Australia. They identified ten types of threatened birds, including one critically endangered yellow-crested cockatoo. Fewer than 7,000 of these cockatoos are left in the wild. Capturing birds to sell increases the chance that wild ones will go **extinct.**

To identify the mystery eggs, Australian forensic scientists compared DNA from shells to DNA sequences in reference databases. These computerized lists contain sequences from known bird species. If scientists found a matching sequence in the databases, they could identify the bird inside the egg.

Forty-three of the eggs could not be identified this way. There were no matching DNA sequences in the databases, because biologists had never studied those bird species. To catch more egg smugglers, more reference sequences must be added to the databases.

An endangered yellow-crested cockatoo.

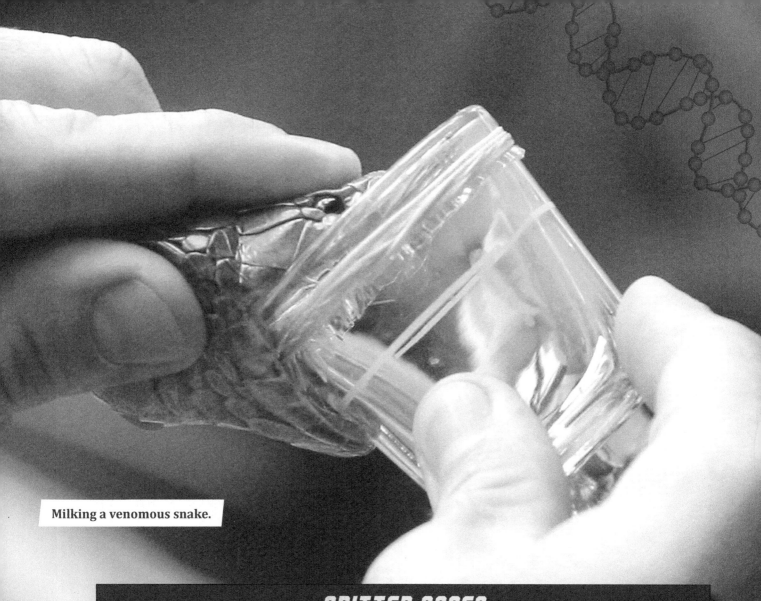

Milking a venomous snake.

The Cobra Catchers

In India, it is illegal to capture, kill, or trade products made from highly endangered Indian cobras. But snake venom is a popular illegal drug, and is worth a lot of money on the black market.

Wildlife traffickers "milk" a snake by forcing it to release venom. Then they dry the venom into crystals and sell it. Before traffickers can be charged, authorities have to prove that the crystals came from an endangered snake.

In the past, this was done using complex chemical reactions, but forensic scientists believed venom crystals might contain snake DNA. In 2012, they tested their hypothesis using three packets of crystals officers had taken from suspected traffickers. All the venom samples contained DNA that matched the reference sequence for Indian cobras. Officers charged the traffickers with hunting an endangered species.

Also known as "white gold," elephant ivory
is used to make a wide range of items.

Elephants and Ivory

Elephants' long teeth, or tusks, are made of ivory. Like gold and gemstones, ivory is highly valued in many cultures. People carve ivory into chopsticks, decorations, and many other items. Unlike elk, which regrow their antlers each year, elephants keep their tusks for life. The only way to collect ivory is to injure or kill an elephant.

CITES banned all trade in elephant ivory in 1989 to protect these vulnerable animals. But demand for ivory has increased, especially in China and Thailand. In the 1990s, smugglers could get US$100 for every kilogram (2 lbs) of illegal ivory. By 2012, the price had risen to US$2,200 per kilogram (2 lbs). This is a big incentive for poachers, especially those from poor African countries where elephants live in the wild.

Elephant tusks are made of ivory, which earns high prices on the black market.

A pile of elephant tusks.

From August 2005 to August 2006, African customs officers seized 12 major shipments of illegal ivory. In total, the shipments included 91 tusks, plus 23,461 kilograms (57,723 lbs) of sliced ivory. It was the second largest seizure of elephant ivory in history, but it was just the tip of the iceberg. Customs officers only detect about 10 percent of all smuggled animal products. That means the amount of ivory in the seized shipments represented as many as 23,000 dead elephants.

The problem was that no one knew which African countries the ivory had come from. Without knowing where elephants were being killed, it was impossible to find and punish the poachers. Once again, forensic scientists believed the answer was in the elephants' DNA.

In their natural habitats, animals tend to stay within a particular area, or home range. They choose mates that live in the same general range. Since animals with different home ranges are not likely to mate, their DNA does not mix. This means that different populations of the same species tend to have different genetic characteristics. Elephants living in Congo, for example, have slightly different DNA than elephants living in Tanzania.

To match ivory to elephant populations, forensic scientists make fingerprints from DNA in the tusks. Next, they do calculations called assignment tests. These tests compare DNA fingerprints of ivory to those of elephants living in different areas. The ivory comes from the elephant population with the most similar DNA.

Results showed that most of the seized ivory came from Zambia, a country in southern Africa. Following the investigation, the Zambian Director of Wildlife was fired. Convicted elephant poachers also received harsher punishments. It is difficult for Zambia and other African countries to enforce their laws, however. There are more poachers hunting elephants than conservation officers working to protect them. The small risk of being caught is nothing compared to the money ivory traffickers can make.

Park guards in Garamba National Park, Democratic Republic of the Congo, Africa.

Speaking for Wildlife

Poachers, smugglers, and traffickers will continue to harm animals as long it makes them rich. The only way to end these illegal activities is to eliminate demand for ivory and other animal products. Until that happens, customs agents and conservation officers will be fighting an uphill battle.

Forensic DNA technology is helping to even their odds. "DNA analysis allows us to investigate cases that we might not have been able to do otherwise," said Bob McClymont, founder of the Alberta Fish and Wildlife's Forensic Laboratory. That means more criminals can be charged.

Bradley White believes DNA fingerprinting also discourages some criminals, who know that forensics could convict them. "I enjoy seeing the work have a real impact on conservation," White said. "Many biologists talk about protecting wildlife, but helping enforce wildlife laws makes a real difference."

Poaching will only stop when poachers and traffickers no longer benefit.

Forensic science gives conservation officers new tools in the fight against wildlife crime.

Officers place a suspect under arrest.

Without DNA fingerprinting, investigators would never have known that Calf 9957 was a wild elk. But Carmichael could not have made this forensic discovery if she didn't already know about animal behavior and genetics. "That knowledge has to come first," she explained. "Wildlife forensics depends on the efforts of ecologists and biologists and geneticists, all of whom increase our understanding of wild species and their DNA. And it's harder for us than for the RCMP or the FBI," she added. "Human victims are all the same species. Wildlife investigations involve thousands of types of plants and animals."

Dr. Burt believed there is another important difference between human crimes and wildlife crimes. Unlike human victims, who can tell their own stories, "Animals can't talk," he said. "They need us to be their voices."

In the case of the kidnapped elk, Hind 154 and Calf 9957 had a whole team of people to speak for them. And despite completing thousands of investigations during his 35 years as a conservation officer, Servetnyk never forgot this one. "This case," he said in 2008, "was the best thing I ever did."

The elk would probably agree.

Turtle Tracks:
Matching Pets to Populations

Endangered turtles are sometimes captured from the wild and sold as pets. This reduces the number of animals living in the wild, increasing their risk of extinction. Sometimes when people tire of their pets, they release them back into the wild. This only helps if turtles are returned to their original location. Turtles released in strange environments may not know how to survive in unfamiliar habitats. The instincts encoded in their DNA do not match the challenges of their new surroundings.

Imagine you are a forensic scientist working in a turtle sanctuary. Your job is to use DNA finger-printing to figure out where pet turtles originally came from. Turtles you match to a population will be returned to their original homes in the wild. Unmatched turtles will be kept in zoos. Three turtles' lives are in your hands. Their DNA fingerprints include two microsatellites, shown in **Table 1**.

Can you figure out where
this turtle came from?

Table 1. DNA Fingerprints for Three Turtles

Turtle's Name ↓	Microsatellite Sizes			
	Microsatellite A		Microsatellite B	
Ella	168	168	197	199
Maeby	166	170	199	201
Fergus	166	172	199	199

Pet owners often release their turtles in unfamiliar environments.

In a wild population, many turtles are related. Therefore, many turtles share microsatellite sizes. A turtle is most likely to come from a population where its microsatellite sizes are common. Forensic scientists measure commonness using percentages. A large percentage means a particular size is often found in that group of turtles. A small percentage means a microsatellite size is rare.

Table 2 shows the percentage for each microsatellite size, measured for two turtle populations: North and South.

Table 2. Microsatellite Sizes*

	Microsatellite A				Microsatellite B		
Population	166	168	170	172	197	199	201
North	0.50	0.38	0.02	0.10	0.33	0.33	0.34
South	0.47	0.18	0.25	0.10	0.20	0.35	0.45

Whole numbers show microsatellite sizes. Decimals show percentages for each size.

Populations are usually made up of related turtles that share some or all of their microsatellite sizes.

To match each turtle to its original population, you need to do an assignment test. This example, for Ella, explains how:

1 — Using **Table 1**, find the microsatellite sizes in Ella's DNA fingerprint.

2 — Using **Table 2**, find the percentages for these sizes among turtles in the North population. Then find the percentages for these sizes among turtles from the South population.

In addition to keeping them as pets, people sometimes kill wild turtles for food

Ella's DNA Fingerprint	168	168	197	199
Percentage from North	0.38	.038	0.33	0.33
Percentage from South	0.18	0.18	0.20	0.35

③ — Next, multiply the percentages from each population:

- Ella — North: 0.38 x 0.38 x 0.33 x 0.33 = 0.015725
- Ella — South: 0.18 x 0.18 x 0.20 x 0.35 = 0.002268

The test result is larger for the North population. This means Ella came from the North population. She can be released into the wild in the northern area.

④ — Follow steps 1–3 to complete the assignment test for Maeby.
Which population does Maeby come from?

⑤ — Follow steps 1–3 to complete the assignment test for Fergus.
Can you be certain where Fergus came from? Where will you send him?

Turn to page 68 to check your answers!

Report A Poacher

REPORT A POACHER
www.reportapoacher.com
1-800-642-3800

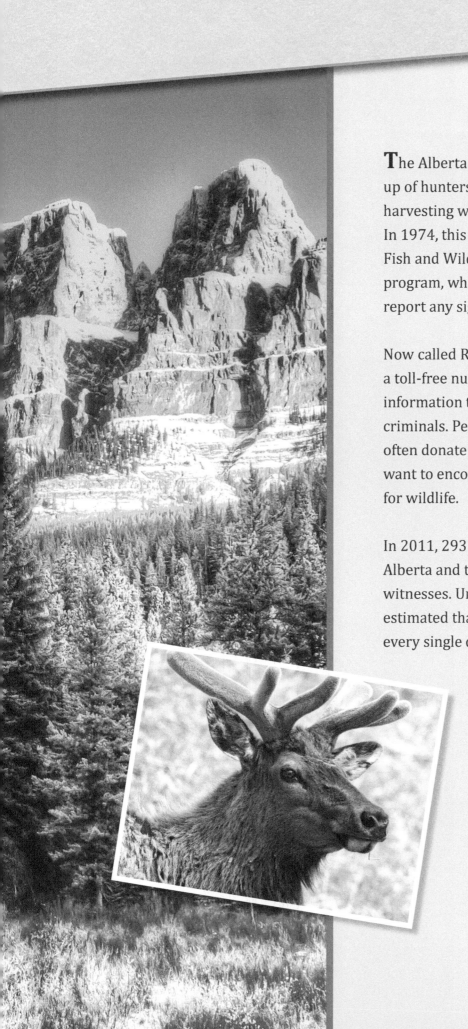

The Alberta Fish & Game Association is made up of hunters and fishermen who believe in harvesting wildlife only according to the law. In 1974, this group joined forces with Alberta Fish and Wildlife to create the Outdoor Observer program, which encouraged ordinary people to report any signs of crimes against wildlife.

Now called Report A Poacher, the program has a toll-free number and offers cash rewards for information that leads to convictions of criminals. People who receive these rewards often donate them back to the program. They want to encourage more witnesses to speak up for wildlife.

In 2011, 293 poachers were arrested in Alberta and the program paid $45,200 to witnesses. Unfortunately, Report A Poacher estimated that eight poaching events happened every single day that year.

To learn more about poaching and how you can help, visit www.reportapoacher.com. If you live outside of Alberta, look for similar programs in your province or state. **And if you witness a crime against wildlife, speak up—give animals a voice.**

Alberta Elk Ranchers

When he made his decision on the case of the kidnapped elk, Judge Marshall said, "So much of the [game farming] industry depends upon the proper enforcement of these regulations and the law-abiding requirement from people who operate." And the vast majority of game ranchers in Canada are law-abiding people. They follow the rules because they love raising elk and want their industry to succeed and grow.

Raising elk is very different from raising sheep or cows. Sheep and cows have depended upon people for thousands of years, and are now different species than their wild ancestors. Ranch elk were wild animals until the 1970s, and remain very similar to elk still living in the wild. As a result, "game producers have a special responsibility to the environment from which their animals ultimately came and to the care of the animals on which they depend."

Alberta elk ranchers take this responsibility very seriously. They feel a strong connection to their land and a deep respect for the animals they raise. They also believe that what they do is important. As Alberta rancher Tina Stewart put it, "I'm proud because the industry is doing good for other people, and that's the whole thing that makes me happy." This "doing good" not only includes providing healthy meat to consumers, but also supporting scientific research that helps us learn more about the benefits of velvet antler.

Elk ranching is a challenging job in many ways, but people who do it love it. "I want to leave the land better than when I got it," rancher Frank McAllister explained. "I'd never give up this life for anything else."

For more information about game ranches, visit:

Alberta Elk Commission
http://albertaelkcommission.com

Canadian Cervid Alliance
http://www.cervid.ca

Glossary

arthritis:
a disease that causes pain and swelling in the joints

bugle:
a squealing noise elk stags make during mating season; bugles start low, become higher pitched, and then drop off

calf:
a baby elk

cell:
the smallest complete piece of a living organism, which both protects DNA and performs a function; skin, muscle, and bone are made up of different types of cells

chromosome:
a package of tightly wound-up DNA found in animal cells; chromosomes come in pairs and an animal inherits one copy of each pair from its mother and father

electrophoresis:
a process for separating pieces of DNA based on their length (size)

enzyme:
a protein that helps chemical reactions occur

extinct:
a species is extinct if there are no individuals left alive anywhere in the world

forensic science:
science used to investigate and solve crimes

hind:
an adult female elk

imprint:
to form a bond between an animal mother and her child;
imprinting allows mothers and children to recognize each other

membrane:
a very thin layer that protects the inside of a cell from everything outside of it

microsatellite:
places in an animal's DNA strands where the base sequences repeat (e.g. ACACACAC)

molecule:
chemicals that make up living creatures, including DNA, proteins, carbohydrates and fats

paternity:
fatherhood

poaching:
the illegal chasing, capturing, injuring, or killing
of wild creatures

Polymerase Chain Reaction (PCR):
a process for copying a specific sequence of DNA,
making it easier to find and measure

purification:
to separate DNA from all of the other molecules
found inside cells

squeeze:
a machine ranchers use to keep animals still
while checking their health or applying ear tags

stag:
an adult male elk

For More Information

Further Reading

Bowers, Vivien. *Crime Scene: How Investigators Use Science to Track Down the Bad Guys.*
Toronto: Maple Tree Press, 2006.

Jackson, Donna M.. *The Wildlife Detectives: How Forensic Scientists Fight Crimes Against Nature.*
New York: Houghton Mifflin Harcourt, 2002.

Rainis, Kenneth G.. *Blood and DNA Evidence: Crime-Solving Science Experiments.*
Berkeley Heights, NJ: Enslow, 2006.

On the Web

Alberta Fish & Game Association
http://www.afga.org/

Alberta Fish and Wildlife
http://esrd.alberta.ca/fish-wildlife/default.aspx

Forensic Science Camp at Trent University
http://forensiccamp.nrdpfc.ca/

TRAFFIC: The Wildlife Trade Monitoring Network
http://www.traffic.org/

Forensics for Kids (a resource list)
http://www.forensicscience.org/resources/forensics-for-kids/

Index

Answers

Answers for Experiment 3

The male lab is the father of Odin and Freya, but cannot be Loki's father. Loki's DNA fingerprint and his curly fur suggest he is probably not a purebred chocolate lab.

The mystery father's DNA fingerprint is:

A		B		C		D		E	
123	?	226	?	178	184	151	153	205	207

For microsatellite A, this father may have a second copy of 123, or a different, unknown size.
For microsatellite B, the puppies tell us he must have size 230 or 232, but we can not be sure which.

Answers for Experiment 4

Maeby's assignment test is 0.001122 for the North population and 0.018506 for the South population. Since the result is much bigger for the South population, Maeby can be released into the wild in the southern area.

Results for Fergus are not clear. His test is 0.005445 for the North population and 0.0057575 for the South population. Because the difference in the results is so small, we can not be sure where Fergus came from. He must be sent to a zoo.

Acknowledgments

This book was a labor of love, and it exists because other people loved it too. Hugs to the lovely and talented ladies of my critique group: Ishta, Halli, Kate, Antje, and Jean, for eagle-eyes and much needed tush-kicking. Deep appreciation to my editor, Karen Latchana Kenney, for finding the bits that made no sense and pushing me to fix them. And to illustrator Nicole Wong and designer Michael Penman, for making my words beautiful.

Most of all, thank you to the passionate and dedicated people who shared their time and expertise during the writing of *Fuzzy Forensics*: Richard and Donna Servetnyk, Ralph and Linda Burt, Simon Taltow, Brad Romaniuk, Jim Mamalis, Janet Smalley, Lisa Monsees, Fernando Rendo, Bradley White, Christopher Kyle, Bob McClymont, Rick Jobin, Michel C. Milinkovitch, and Greg Wilson. I'm honored that I was able to tell your stories.

About the Author

L. E. Carmichael never outgrew that stage of childhood when nothing's more fun than amazing your friends (and correcting your teachers!) with your stockpile of weird and wonderful facts. While in graduate school at the University of Alberta, Carmichael completed DNA fingerprinting for 15 wildlife forensic cases and testified as an expert witness.

Since completing her PhD, she's written children's books about everything from health conditions to hybrid cars. Her previous book with Ashby-BP, *Fox Talk: How Some Very Special Animals Helped Scientists Understand Communication*, answers the eternal question, "What does the fox say?"

You can visit her online at **www.lecarmichael.ca**

Designer & Illustrator

PenmanWorks is an innovative writing, editing, and design company focused on children's publishing. Specialties include picture books and nonfiction titles for elementary/middle school readers.

Founded by renowned children's book veteran, Michael Penman, our background includes 15 years' of industry experience, over 30 books/1 million copies in print, 50+ publishing awards, co-development of the *Adventures of Riley* children's brand, and a proven commitment to our clients and their project goals.

Find out more at: **www.PenmanWorks.com**

Nicole M. Wong is a science illustrator based in Brooklyn by way of San Francisco. She is fascinated by animals and their interactions, imagining how they experience the world, and examining the ways in which humans relate to nature. Some fun jobs in her past include studying wild monkeys in Bolivia, and reconstructing an ancient Roman mural for the American Museum of Natural History.

She hopes her art entices viewers to learn something new, and encourages people of all ages to turn an inquisitive eye to this complex world around us!

Find out more at:
www.nicolemwong.com

photo Credits

Cover and interior design by Michael Penman/PenmanWorks, www.PenmanWorks.com
Indexing by Dan Connolly, www.wfwbooks.com
Illustrations used with permission by Nicole Wong, www.nicolemwong.com

Photography used with permission from Shutterstock and its respective Copyright holders: Carol Mellema, Nicemonkey, Nancy Catherine Walker, Urszula Czapla, Le Do, Martin Pateman, wavebreakmedia, BGSmith, Matt Gibson, COSfoto, ChrisVanLennepPhoto, Bruce Raynor, Maksim Toome, Karin Hildebrand Lau, visceralimage, jps, worldinmyeyes.pl, koosen, Steve Bower, Protasov AN, Ai825, Pictureguy, tratong, Sarah Jessup, Gregory Johnston, Holly Kuchera, dimitris_k, Shawn Hempel, isak55, Vit Kovalcik, kubais, Guido Akster, Nathan B Dappen, luchschen, Alex Staroseltsev, Andrey_Popov, OPOLJA, JPagetRFPhotos, ARTSILENSE, Ant Clausen, Susan Schmitz, outdoorsman, Attila JANDI, Steve Heap, jazzia, Monika Wisniewska, riekephotos, tratong, mark Higgins, Artem Efimov, Alberto Tirado, KellyNelson, Lagui, javarman, Johan W. Elzenga, Svetlana Foote, Rudi Hulshof, arturasker, Jakkrit Orrasri, sgm, Marsan, Ivan Smuk, Mr. SUTTIPON YAKHAM, White Room, Alexandra Lande, EBFoto, Domenic Gareri, Lisa F. Young, Aspen Photo, A.von Dueren, Vasiliy Koval, Mark Caunt, Terry Honeycutt, Sergey Skleznev, kowit sitthi, bikeriderlondon, Curioso, smikeymikey1, vitstudio

Additional images and photography used with permission from: FRANS LANTING, MINT IMAGES/ Science Photo Library, Report A Poacher, Donna Servetnyk, Linda Burt, Brian Dust, L.E. Carmichael, The Australian Customs and Border Protection Service, Dr. Christopher Kyle, Richard Jervis/Artistic Creations, Alberta Justice and Solicitor General, John J. Cox and Songdog Photography, US Geological Survey - Northern Divide Bear Project, Bradley White, S. Neil Moore, Extravectors.com.

ISBN-10:   1-928005-03-9
ISBN-13:   978-1-928005-03-2
BISAC: Juvenile Nonfiction : Law & Crime
            Law : Forensic Science
            Juvenile Nonfiction : Animals - Animal Welfare

Alberta Government

Published in Canada and the United States by Ashby-BP Publishing.
Printed in the United States of America.

Remember to be a Safe CSI

Read all instructions and warnings before beginning an experiment.
Check with an adult before you start.
Do not smell or taste rubbing alcohol or any mixtures that contain it.
Always clean up after your experiments.

Scientists don't take risks. Neither should you.

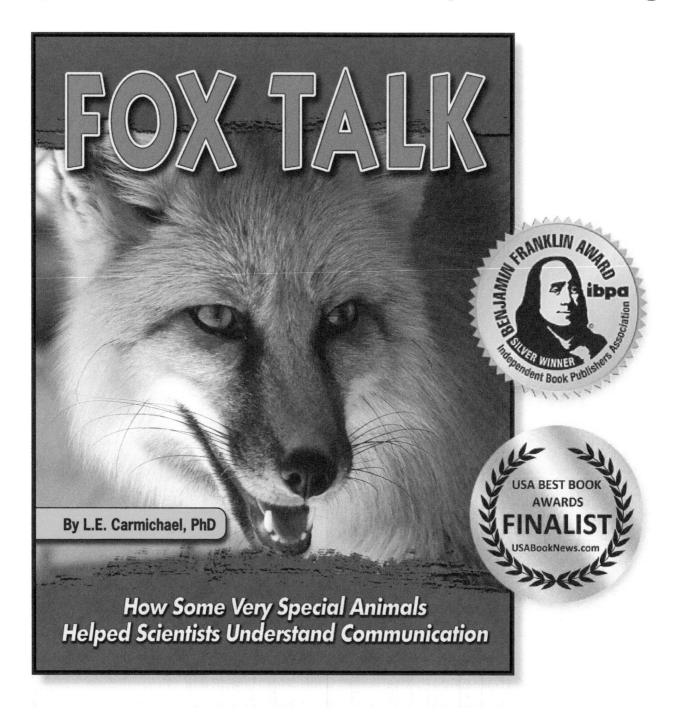

CPSIA information can be obtained at www.ICGtesting.com
Printed in the USA
BVOW11s1614131114

374676BV00001BA/1/P

9 781928 005032